973 Bright
American fun facts

WITHDRAWN

8215
Mentor Public Library

Mentor Public Library
12/16/2015

© Auzou Publishing, Paris (France), 2015 (English version)

General Manager: Gauthier Auzou
Senior Editor: Marine Courvoisier
Production: Jean-Christophe Collett
Graphic Design: Eloïse Jensen
English Version Editor: Christopher Murray
ISBN: 978-2-9237-3238-7
Printed and bound in China, February 2015

All rights reserved. No part of this book may be used or reproduced in any form or by any means, electronic or mechanical, including photocopying, recording, or by any information storage and retrieval system, without permission in writing from the publisher.

AMERICAN

Fun Facts

By J. E. Bright

Illustrations by Medhi Dewalle

AUZOU

CONTENTS

1. HOW WAS MICKEY MOUSE CREATED?

In 1928, Walt Disney asked his chief animator Ub Iwerks to sketch ideas for a new character. Iwerks drew cats and frogs and cows and dogs, but Disney didn't think they'd found their new star. Then one day a mouse visited Disney at his desk and he fed it crumbs.

So Disney collaborated with Iwerks to create a mouse character. To make animating it easier, Iwerks designed Mickey's body, head, and ears in big circles. Disney planned to name the mouse Mortimer, but his wife Lillian decided on a less formal name: Mickey.

Disney and Iwerks co-directed a short cartoon, which Iwerks animated with the assistance of Hugh Harman and Rudolf Ising. It took them six weeks to draw the entire film. In 1928, along with his girlfriend Minnie, Mickey Mouse's first starring role in *Plane Crazy* was released to the world.

It flopped with audiences.

Disney produced a second Mickey cartoon called *The Gallopin' Gaucho*. Iwerks animated it. That second short also got little attention. However, their third cartoon, *Steamboat Willie*, broke through in a big way. It helped that they added the innovation of sound.

Mickey Mouse became an international superstar, speaking with the friendly voice of Walt Disney.

2. WHAT WAS THE FIRST VIDEO GAME SYSTEM SOLD IN AMERICA?

In 1951, television engineer Ralph Baer had an idea for an interactive game using a TV screen. By 1967, he and his associates figured out how to control parts of a television's display screen with video signals. They created a collection of games that showed off their new technology.

Electronics company Magnavox invested in Baer's invention, and released the first home video game console in 1972. They called it the Odyssey.

The graphics were limited to a few basic shapes. The set came with accessories, including plastic overlays that were taped to the television screen to add color and backgrounds to the plain black-and-white movable shapes in the game. Other game cartridges required dice, paper cards, money, or plastic chips and other pieces to play. The scores of games had to be kept on a pad of paper.

Ralph Baer was awarded the National Medal of Technology in 2006, and inducted into the National Inventors Hall of Fame in 2010.

3. WHY DO AMERICANS CELEBRATE THANKSGIVING?

When the Pilgrims arrived from Europe on the Mayflower and founded a colony in Plymouth, Massachusetts in November 1620, they weren't ready for the brutal winter. Nearly half of the settlers died. Assisted by Wampanoag Indians, the survivors enjoyed a bountiful harvest the following summer, and celebrated with a three-day feast, starting on December 13, 1621. It's probable that they ate turkey, goose, duck, venison, berries, corn, and pumpkin.

George Washington, the first president of the United States, declared that America should hold a Thanksgiving celebration nationwide on November 26, 1789. However, November 26 wasn't an official holiday. The various colonies and states celebrated on different days every year.

In 1863, President Abraham Lincoln proclaimed that the last Thursday of November was a national Day of Thanksgiving. He was hoping to create unity between the battling Northern and Southern states during the third year of the Civil War, but the war also prevented the holiday from being universally celebrated. President Franklin D. Roosevelt signed a congressional resolution in 1941, officially declaring Thanksgiving Day as a national holiday every fourth Thursday in November.

4. WHICH AMERICAN MOVIE ACTOR HAD THE MOST LEADING ROLES IN FEATURE FILMS?

According to the *Guinness Book of World Records*, the great western actor John Wayne received top billing in more feature films than any other movie star. In his career, he played the lead role in 142 of the approximately 175 movies in which he appeared.

He was born Marion Mitchell Morrison on May 26, 1907, and his tough, conservative image, calm voice, and swaggering walk made him an enduring American icon of cowboy masculinity.

John Wayne won the Academy Award for Best Actor in a Leading Role in 1969 for *True Grit*. He died on June 11, 1979, leaving behind an enduring and impressive legacy in film.

5. DO MORE AMERICANS HAVE CATS OR DOGS AS PETS?

The Humane Society of the United States released estimates in 2012 that showed approximately 83.3 million dogs were owned in America. Some 47% of households had at least one dog. Most owners only had one dog, at 70%, while 20% had two, and 10% had three dogs or more. Approximately 20% of dogs had been adopted from a shelter. People owned male or female dogs in nearly equal numbers.

But cats win. Nearly 96 million cats are kept as pets in America. Forty-six percent of households with cats had only one, while 31% had two, and 24% had three or more. A little more than 25% of pet cats had been adopted from a shelter. While 73% of owners chose a female feline companion, 62% hat a male cat.

6. HOW DID THE UNITED STATES OF AMERICA GET ITS NAME?

Around 1500 AD, an explorer and map maker named Amerigo Vespucci (1454-1512) traveled to the West Indies and Brazil, voyaging along the coast and demonstrating that the land was not part of Asia, but rather an entirely separate continent.

Using Vespucci's reports, Martin Waldseemüller made a map of the world in 1507, and named the new continent America, using the Latin, feminized version of Vespucci's first name. The name stuck, and was even expanded into North and South America as maps improved.

The "United States" part of the name was inspired by Thomas Jefferson. In 1776, he wrote the phrase "United States of America" in a rough draft of the Declaration of Independence. The next year, the Articles of Confederation, an early document of cooperation between the 13 American colonies, officially decreed, "the Stile of this Confederacy shall be 'The United States of America.'"

The Articles were eventually replaced by the Constitution, which has a preamble beginning, "We the people of the United States. . ."

7. WHAT ARE THE BIGGEST AND SMALLEST STATES BY AREA?

The largest state by area is Alaska, with 663,268 square miles of land. Alaska has the fourth fewest people of any state: about 732,000 people call it home.

Texas is the largest state by area in the contiguous United States, since Alaska is not physically connected to the rest of the country.

The smallest state by area is Rhode Island, with 1,214 square miles of land. It has a population of about a million people.

8. WHO WAS THE FIRST AMERICAN PRESIDENT TO APPEAR ON TELEVISION?

Franklin Delano Roosevelt was the first president to appear on TV. His dedication speech at the opening ceremonies of the World's Fair in New York City was filmed in black-and-white and broadcast on April 30, 1939. His audience was small, since commercial television was introduced to the public at that same fair.

The first president to give a nationally televised speech from the White House was Harry S. Truman on October 5, 1947. To help hungry Europeans in the aftermath of World War II, the president requested that citizens conserve grain.

On June 6, 1955, Dwight D. Eisenhower made an appearance at the United States Military Academy in West Point to celebrate his class's 40th reunion. The news coverage of the event was the first time an American president appeared in color on TV.

9. WHAT ARE FIVE OF THE NICKNAMES OF NEW YORK CITY?

The Big Apple

A reporter for *The Morning Telegraph* in the 1920s overheard stable hands describing New York City's racetracks by calling them "the big apple"—a compliment to the top billing of New York's racing. The phrase resurfaced in the 1930s when jazz musicians referred to the incomparable music scene in the city. In the 1970s, an advertising campaign attached the nickname to New York City forever.

Gotham

Native New Yorker and writer Washington Irving heard a story about a tiny town in England called Gotham, where the people pretended to be insane. Irving satirically called New York City "Gotham" in an 1807 essay in *Salmagundi* magazine.

The City That Never Sleeps

Perhaps because it was the first city illuminated by electric light, "The City That Never Sleeps" has been a nickname for New York City since 1912, when it appeared in print in the *Fort Wayne* News. The phrase's fame was cemented in the 1977 song "Theme from New York, New York."

Capital of the World

Although mentioned by writer E. B. White in his 1949 essay, "Here Is New York," and repeated by Pope John Paul II in 1979, this nickname's main popularity came at the insistence of Mayor Rudolph Giuliani in the 1990s.

The City

Because New York is the most populous city in America, and is so important in the realms of finance, technology, media, fashion, art and culture, sometimes it's called simply "The City."

10. WHAT IS THE OLDEST CITY IN AMERICA?

In 1513, explorer Juan Ponce de Leon sailed from a settlement in Puerto Rico, searching nearby islands for the Fountain of Youth. He didn't find any magical waters, but he claimed the fertile coastline he discovered for Spain and named it "Florida." A city named St. Augustine was founded near de Leon's landing site in 1565. In comparison, the first successful English settlement in the Americas was at Jamestown, Virginia in 1607. St. Augustine is considered the country's oldest continuous settlement. It's located 38 miles southeast of Jacksonville, Florida's largest and most populous city.

11. WHY WERE THE NATIVE AMERICANS ORIGINALLY CALLED INDIANS?

When Christopher Columbus made landfall in the Antilles archipelago islands in 1492, he mistakenly believed that he had found a route to the Indian Ocean, and therefore called the people already present, "Indians." He was actually in the Caribbean.

Although Columbus' mistake was discovered quickly, the name persisted until the present day. The inaccuracy carried over into geography, too: the islands of the Caribbean are known as the West Indies.

12. WHAT IS THE MOST POPULAR SPORT IN AMERICA?

In polls, nearly 39% of sports enthusiasts choose the National Football League as their favorite sports to watch. Multiple Super Bowls have broken records for most watched television events in history, with Super Bowl XLVIII hitting 111.5 million viewers. NFL games have on average more fans in their stadiums than any other sports league in the world. Although when it comes to active players, football comes in fourth, with 8.9 million participants.

Basketball is in second place in terms of popularity, with more than 15 percent of Americans choosing the National Basketball Association as their favorite professional sports league. Nearly 24 million people play basketball regularly, making it the most played sport. In third place is baseball. Less than 15 percent of people polled chose Major League Baseball as their favorite professional league to watch. Participants around the country numbered about 23 million.

13. HOW MANY PLAYERS ARE ON A FOOTBALL TEAM?

The game of football is played between two teams who are each allowed to have a maximum of 11 players on the field at a time.

Teams are penalized if they play more than 11. There is no penalty for having fewer than 11, although following a change of possession or a timeout, the referee will hold the ball out of play until the offense has 11 players in its huddle.

Between downs, coaches may replace any number of their players.

Each team in the National Football League may have exactly 53 players on their active roster. Seven players must be held in reserve for each game, and only 46 may dress and prepare to play on a given game day, expanded from 45 in 2011.

14. WHICH NATIVE AMERICAN WAS VOTED THE GREATEST ATHLETE OF THE 20TH CENTURY?

James Francis "Jim" Thorpe was a versatile American athlete of both Native American and European heritage. Born on May 28, 1888, he was raised in Oklahoma with the Sac and Fox Nation. His Native American name is Wa-Tho-Huk, which translates as "Bright Path."

Thorpe gained notoriety playing college football. Thorpe participated in the Olympic Games in Stockholm, Sweden, and won gold medals for the pentathlon and decathlon. Unfortunately, his Olympic titles were taken from him when it was discovered he played baseball semi-professionally, violating old, strict requirements that Olympians must be amateurs.

In 1913, Thorpe joined the New York Giants baseball team. He then switched to playing professional football in the league that would become the NFL, even acting as president of the league from 1920 to 1921. Thorpe also played basketball with a traveling team of Native American players. Thorpe died on March 28, 1953.

In 1983, the International Olympic Committee restored his Olympic medals.

In a 2001 ABC Wide World of Sports poll, Thorpe was chosen the Athlete of the Century.

15. WHERE WAS THE FIRST WORLD SERIES HELD?

The first championship series between baseball leagues was held in 1884 at the Polo Grounds in New York City. The New York Metropolitan Club of the American Association lost to the Providence Grays of the National League in three games. It was the first competition called the World Series. In 1891, the American Association stopped operating.

A decade later, the American League was formed. The first modern World Series against the National League was held in 1903, with the Boston Americans battling the Pittsburgh Pirates. The first three games were played at Huntington Avenue American League Base Ball Grounds in Boston, Massachusetts. The middle four games took place at Exposition Park in Pittsburgh, Pennsylvania, with the final game back at Huntington Avenue, where the Boston Americans won the series.The Boston Americans became the Boston Red Sox a few years later.

16. WHAT IS THE TALLEST MOUNTAIN IN THE UNITED STATES?

With a peak elevation of 20,237 feet above sea level, Mount McKinley is the tallest mountain in North America and in the United States.

Located in Alaska, it was named Denali by the Koyukon Athabaskan indigenous people who lived around it. In 1917, it was renamed to honor President William McKinley, who was assassinated in 1901 after only six months in office. The state of Alaska continues to refer to the mountain as Denali, although the United States government, which owns the national park in which it's located, officially calls it Mount McKinley.

Because Alaska is not directly connected to the rest of the country, it's worth mentioning that Mount Whitney has the highest peak in the "lower 48 states," with an elevation of 14,505 feet. Mount Whitney is located in California, where it is flanked by the Sequoia National Park and the Inyo National Forest. It may be the most climbed mountain summit in the United States.

17. WHAT IS THE LARGEST ANIMAL IN AMERICA?

Sometimes incorrectly called a buffalo, the American bison is the largest living animal in the USA.

There are two types of bison. The Plains variety has a rounded hump. The Wood bison is larger and has a boxy hump. An adult bison's body varies from 6.6 to 11.5 feet long, with the tail adding anywhere from 12 to 36 extra inches. A full-grown bison can sometimes grow as tall as 6 feet, measured from the ground to the top of the shoulder, and have horns up to 2 feet long. The biggest bison bull ever recorded weighed 2,800 pounds!

Before the 19th century, herds totaling 50 million bison migrated across the vast American grasslands. Disease and hunting nearly forced the bison into extinction, but the majestic animal now has a stable population protected in zoos and national parks.

18. WHAT LEGENDARY MONSTER IS SAID TO LIVE IN OREGON'S CRATER LAKE?

Located in Oregon, Crater Lake partly fills a nearly 2,148-foot-deep, 6-mile-wide caldera (volcanic crater) that was formed when the volcano Mount Mazama erupted violently and then collapsed.

The deepest lake in the United States (1,943 feet), and among the top 10 deepest in the world, Crater Lake is renown for its clear, deep blue water. No rivers flow in or out-the lake is fed by rain and snowmelt. There are two islands in the lake: Phantom Ship and Wizard Island.

Crater Lake is sacred to the Klamath tribe, whose ancestors may have witnessed the collapse of Mount Mazama 7,700 years ago. In Klamath legends, Mount Mazama's awesome explosion was the result of a battle between Llao, the god of the underworld, and Skell, the sky god. From the terrible destruction of their war was born Crater Lake. Llao remained as chief spirit of the lake, the master of many lesser spirits who appeared as animals. One dangerous spirit took the form of a gigantic crayfish, known to snatch unsuspecting people from the caldera's rim and drag them down to drown.

19. WHICH VOLCANOES HAVE ERUPTED IN THE UNITED STATES SINCE 1900?

In Hawaii, the massive Mauna Loa volcano has gushed out lava 15 times, most recently in 1984. Rising from its flank is Kilauea, the world's most active volcano, which has erupted without interruption since 1983.

In Alaska, the Aleutian arc is a string of fiery volcanoes. The largest eruption in the world since 1900 happened at Novarupta in 1912. Trident Volcano erupted intermittently from 1953 through 1960. Augustine Volcano erupted in 1935, 1963-64, 1976, and 1986. Mount Redoubt erupted for the fourth time this century in 1989. Mount Spurr, the Aleutian volcano with the highest elevation, exploded from its Crater Peak in 1992.

In California, Lassen Peak had a series of spectacular eruptions between 1914 and 1917.

In the state of Washington, Mount St. Helens erupted in 1980, causing more damage to lives and property than any other volcano in America's history.

20. WHERE IS THE COLDEST PLACE IN AMERICA?

Nowhere in the USA is colder than Alaska. Prospect Creek, a tiny Alaskan pipeline pumping settlement near the Arctic Circle, had the coldest temperature ever recorded in America, dropping to a frigid -80 degrees Fahrenheit in 1971. No people currently live at the Prospect Creek camp, although bears and bald eagles survive in the extreme temperatures of the area. The official lowest temperature ever recorded in the lower 48 states of America, was -70° F in 1954 at Rogers Pass, Montana, a trail through the Rocky Mountains along the Continental Divide.

21. WHAT WAS THE FIRST NATIONAL PARK IN AMERICA?

In 1872, President Ulysses S. Grant signed a bill establishing Yellowstone, considered the first national park in the world.

Located mostly in Wyoming, the park covers 3,472 square miles. The park's highest point is Eagle Peak, at 11,358 feet above sea level. Reese Creek is its lowest point at 5,282 feet. Along with its spectacular lakes, rivers, waterfalls, canyons and mountains, Yellowstone is famous for its geothermal activity, especially Old Faithful geyser. Yellowstone Lake covers the Yellowstone Caldera, the largest active volcano on the continent.

Hundreds of animals live in the park, some of which are threatened or endangered. There are herds of bison and elk, along with wolves and bears, including grizzly bears.

22. WHICH STATE HAS THE MOST TORNADOES IN THE WORLD?

The United States has more tornadoes every year than any other country in the world. Though no state is completely free of tornado danger, including Alaska and Hawaii, most of the storms spin in the middle of the continent between the Rocky Mountains and the Appalachian Mountains, in the stretch of land called Tornado Alley.

Texas reports the most tornadoes annually, with an average of 139 per year, followed by Oklahoma with 57, Kansas and Florida tied with 55, and Nebraska with 45.

23. WHAT IS THE TALLEST SKYSCRAPER IN AMERICA?

The tallest skyscraper in the U.S., as of 2013, is One World Trade Center in New York City. Its completed spire rises to a height of 1,776 feet, which is a symbolic reference to the year of the signing of the Declaration of Independence. One WTC is the fourth-tallest building in the world, and the tallest in the Western Hemisphere. If the spire isn't included, however, Chicago's Willis Tower has a taller roof and higher occupied floor.

24. WHAT IS THE COLOR OF SAN FRANCISCO'S GOLDEN GATE BRIDGE?

The Golden Gate Bridge is painted orange vermilion, also known as "International Orange."
The characteristic color was chosen because it complements the beautiful natural cliffs and rolling hills on either side, while standing out against the blue-grays of the ocean and sometimes foggy skies, providing extra visibility for ships.
The bridge spans the entrance from the Pacific Ocean to San Francisco Bay—a strait named "Chrysopylae," or Golden Gate by engineers in the U.S. Army around 1846. So the name of the bridge refers to the name of the strait, not the bridge's color. It's not gold.

25. WHO SCULPTED THE STATUE OF LIBERTY?

The "Statue of Liberty Enlightening the World," better known as the Statue of Liberty, was designed and sculpted by a French artist named Frédéric Auguste Bartholdi, who lived from 1834 to 1904.

The statue of a robed woman holding up a torch stands at 151 feet and 1 inch high, with the torch reaching a height of 305 feet and 1 inch. There are rumors that Bartholdi based the statue's face on his mother's.

In 1886, it was raised on its pedestal on Bedloe's Island in New York Harbor, and officially presented as a gift of friendship between the French and American people. The statue was the tallest structure in New York until 1929, when the Empire State building rose Higher.

The Statue of Liberty is recognized worldwide as an enduring symbol of democracy and freedom.

26. WHICH TWO CITIES DID HISTORIC ROUTE 66 CONNECT?

Route 66 (also known as U.S. Highway 66) was established on November 11, 1926, with road signs being placed by the next year. It was one of the earliest American highways.

Originally, the road began in Chicago, Illinois, and traveled through Missouri, Kansas, Oklahoma, Texas, New Mexico, and Arizona, before reaching its endpoint in Los Angeles, California. It crossed 2,448 miles. Over the years, Route 66 was improved, making more direct connections or providing detours around slow city traffic. In 1936, the California side was extended from Los Angeles to Santa Monica, where it connected to the Pacific Coast Highway.

During the Dust Bowl era of the 1930s, Route 66 held special importance for the migrants who moved west in search of a better life.

Eventually, the wide Interstate Highway System was built, making the narrower Route 66 irrelevant. Route 66 fell into disuse, and was officially removed from the United States Highway System in 1985.

Portions of the road have been designated a National Scenic Byway, appearing on maps and signs as "Historic Route 66."

27. WHY IS THE UNITED STATES DOLLAR CALLED THE DOLLAR?

In 1785, the Continental Congress of the United States created a new currency, the U.S. dollar.
But where did they get the word? Dollar comes from the German word *thaler*, a shortened version of *Joachimsthaler*, a coin created from silver mined in the 16th century in St. Joachim's Valley in what is now the Czech Republic. *Thaler* was translated into many languages, such as *daler* in Swedish, *talar* in Polish, *tallero* in Italian, *dare* in Persian, and *daler* in Danish. Eventually, the English picked up the word as dollar.

28. WHAT IS AMERICA'S MOST RECOGNIZED BUSINESS LOGO?

In 2013, the editors of *Complex* magazine chose the Nike Swoosh as the most recognized logo in the USA.

The Nike logo was created in 1971 by student designer Carolyn Davidson, who was paid $35 for the rights to the design. The shape symbolizes the wing on a famous statue of Nike, the Greek goddess of victory, echoing a fluid, fast movement. The logo was chosen by Nike co-founder Philip Knight, who reportedly said, "I don't love it, but it will grow on me." The new design was called "the strip" at first, but by the time it debuted on of athletic shoe in 1972, it was known as the "Swoosh."

The Swoosh was registered as a trademark in 1995 and has become the central identity of Nike, so much so that the company removed the Nike name from the design, leaving only Davidson's symbol as the company's logo.

29. WHO IS THE ONLY AMERICAN WOMAN TO APPEAR ON PAPER MONEY?

The first woman to be featured on U.S. currency was Martha Washington, the wife of President George Washington, and the original First Lady of the United States. She appeared on the $1 Silver Certificate in 1886, 1891, and 1896. She is still the only American woman to have been portrayed on paper money in this country.

30. WHERE DID THE COFFEE COMPANY STARBUCKS GET ITS NAME?

Starbucks was founded in Seattle, Washington in 1971 by three academics: history teacher Zev Siegel, writer Gordon Bowker, and English teacher Jerry Baldwin.

But how did they come up with the famous name? The trio of founders considered all kinds of names at first, and almost went with Cargo House. Then someone suggested that they use a name beginning with the sound "ST," which seemed powerful. When Bowker saw an antique map of the Cascade mountains, he spotted an old mining town named Starbo. That led him to remember the name of the first mate in the whaling novel *Moby-Dick*, who was named Starbuck.

The name evoked the adventure of sailing on the high seas, but it was more about the sound than any direct reference to the character in the famous novel. Bowker admitted that Starbuck, the first mate of the Pequod, wasn't known for loving coffee in the book. It was in the movie that Starbuck drank coffee constantly.

31. FOR WHAT PROFESSION WERE BLUE JEANS FIRST USED?

In 1853, Bavarian-born Levi Strauss was working with his brothers at the family dry-goods store in New York City when news about the California Gold Rush fired his imagination. He moved to San Francisco to open a business for the influx of settlers there.With Strauss' brothers supplying goods from New York, Levi and his brother-in-law David Stern built a very successful store in San Francisco and renamed their business Levi Strauss & Co.

Meanwhile, a tailor named Jacob Davis had invented a way to strengthen trousers by placing metal rivets in the denim material. He needed a partner to manufacture the pants, and proposed the idea to Strauss, from whom he had been buying his cloth for years. Strauss agreed, and together they shared the patent for putting rivets in men's work pants in 1873.

At the time, Strauss and Davis called their reinforced trousers "waist overalls" or "overalls." The term "jeans" wasn't used until the 1960s.

The pants were an instant hit with the workmen in the area, especially San Francisco's many miners who had arrived for the Gold Rush. The "waist overalls" quickly became popular with other working men, including cowboys, teamsters, lumberjacks, and farmers.

32. WHO CREATED MCDONALD'S?

Brothers Richard and Maurice McDonald moved with their family from New Hampshire to California in the 1920s, where they worked as handymen at movie studios. In 1937, their father Patrick McDonald opened a food stand called the Airdrome on Route 66 near the Monrovia airport.

The brothers simplified the menu to hamburgers, cheeseburgers, French fries, shakes, soft drinks, and apple pie. They set up their kitchen and customer service to ensure maximum efficiency. By 1948, their restaurant was renamed McDonald's.

Four years later, the brothers added two 25-foot yellow sheet-metal structures trimmed in neon light they called the Golden Arches.

In 1954, Ray Kroc, a milkshake machine salesman, offered to help expand McDonald's with franchises across the country. He opened his first McDonald's restaurant in Des Plaines, Illinois, near Chicago. By 1958, Kroc had franchised 34 restaurants. By 1959, that number had increased to 102.

Ray Kroc bought the company from the McDonald brothers in 1961 for $2.7 million dollars.

In 2012, McDonald's revenues reached $27 billion annually, with 34,000 restaurants worldwide.

33. WHERE WAS COCA-COLA CREATED?

Confederate Colonel John Stith Pemberton (1831-1888) created a recipe for French Wine Coca at a drugstore called Pemberton's Eagle Drug and Chemical House in Columbus, Georgia.

In 1885, Pemberton registered his nerve tonic, but had to change the recipe the next year when his county passed prohibition laws. He took alcohol out of the formula and called it Coca-Cola.

The first sale of Coca-Cola was at Jacob's Pharmacy in Atlanta in 1886. It was initially sold as a patent medicine for five cents at soda fountains. Pemberton claimed Coca-Cola cured many diseases.

34. HOW MANY CHICKENS ARE EATEN EVERY YEAR IN AMERICA?

In the 1900s, eating chicken was a typical meal only on Sundays. In the next century, chicken consumption in the U.S. greatly increased until poultry became part of everyday meals.

In 2013, 8,648,756 chickens were slaughtered for sale.

According to the Wing Report from the National Chicken Council in 2014, Americans ate 1.25 billion chicken wings during Super Bowl XLVIII alone.

35. WHAT IS AMERICA'S FAVORITE KIND OF CHEESE?

Thanks to America's consumption of pizza and other Italian-inspired foods, mozzarella's popularity is far ahead of its cheese competitors. In a survey of 36,000 menu items in restaurants in America, mozzarella was the leading cheese, listed in 21% of all foods on the menu.

Mozzarella is often eaten as a cheese sticks appetizer, too, and as a string cheese snack in homes. American cheese is popular for burgers, and cheddar, provolone, and Swiss are used most often for sandwiches, while jack or cheddar cheeses are the choice for Mexican-inspired foods such as quesadillas and tacos. However, mozzarella remains America's favorite cheese overall.

36. WHO WERE THE FIRST EUROPEANS TO ENCOUNTER NATIVE AMERICANS?

Europeans may have first made contact with Native Americans nearly 500 years before Christopher Columbus reached the Americas. According to Old Norse sagas, Icelander Thorvald Eriksson, the son of famous explorer Erik the Red and brother to explorer Leif Eriksson, set off on an expedition to Vinland, in present-day Newfoundland, Canada. As he was unloading his boat, a native shot Thorvald in the belly with an arrow. His last words were, "This is a rich country we have found." Along with possibly being one of the first Europeans to meet a Native American, Thorvald was perhaps the first European to be killed by one. He also may have been the first European buried in North America.

37. WHICH STATE HAS THE ONLY ROYAL PALACE IN THE USA?

Iolani Palace, located in the capitol district of downtown Honolulu, Hawaii, is the only palace built for royalty that is now in the United States.

In 1882, the palace was constructed by King David Kalakaua, the last king of Hawaii. It functioned as the government seat for the Kingdom of Hawaii.

The palace remained a royal residence until the Hawaiian monarchy was overthrown in 1893. The ruler at the time, Queen Lili'uokalani, was deposed. Two years later, she was imprisoned in Iolani Palace for eight months, charged with treason for trying to restore Hawaii's sovereignty. In 1978, Iolani Palace opened to the public as a museum. It's listed as a National Historic Landmark on the National Register of Historic Places.

38. WHAT WAS THE ORIGINAL NAME OF ATLANTA, GEORGIA?

In 1837, a stake was driven into the ground in Georgia marking the end point of a new train line called the Western and Atlantic Railroad. John Thrasher built a general store at the location, along with a few homes. He called the settlement Thrasherville.
As the settlement grew, it came to be known as Terminus, which means "end of the line."
In 1842, Governor Wilson Lumpkin requested that the community be named after his daughter Martha. Terminus became Marthasville.
J. Edgar Thomson, the Chief Engineer of the Georgia Railroad, suggested in 1845 that Marthasville be renamed Atlantica-Pacifica. The residents approved, but shortened it to Atlanta.
The town was incorporated as Atlanta in 1847.

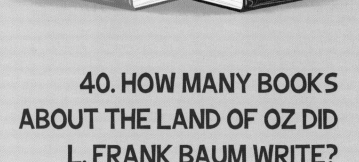

39. WHAT WAS THE FIRST SPORT PLAYED IN AMERICA?

Perhaps as early as 1100 AD, Native Americans played a game between teams that used a small ball hurled and caught with a long, hand-held stick with a mesh pouch on one end. Played as a contact sport, the game had deep spiritual significance for the players as serious warriors, with the goal to bring honor to themselves and their tribes.
In 1637, French Jesuit missionary Jean de Brébeuf witnessed Iroquois tribesmen playing the sport in present-day New York. He was the first European to write about the game, and he called it "la crosse," which means "the stick."

40. HOW MANY BOOKS ABOUT THE LAND OF OZ DID L. FRANK BAUM WRITE?

L. Frank Baum's original book about the Land of Oz, *The Wonderful Wizard of Oz*, was published in 1900. It's often considered to be the first original American fairytale. The book was wildly popular with children in the U.S. and around the world, and so Baum eventually wrote 13 sequels about the adventures of Dorothy and the other characters adventures in the magical world of Oz.

DEC 17 2010